THE TREE of KNOWLEDGE

by

ALVIN BOYD KUHN

[1947]

Reprint 2011

©2011. Zuubooks.com. All Rights Reserved. No reproduction of this book may be stored in an electronic device or reprinted without the written consent of the author. United States Copyright and International law applies. ZuuBooks specialize in offering rare printed and ebooks for affordable prices. For more information on our products and services for authors please contact us at ilifeebooks@gmail.com

This has been a ZuuBooks.com Publication. For New and Classic titles in Audiobooks, ebooks, and Paperback please visit us at www.zuuBooks.com

Authors who are interested in publishing and distributing their works can contact us at ilifeebooks@gmail.com

THE TREE *of* KNOWLEDGE

by

ALVIN BOYD KUHN

[1947]

Reprint 2011

THE TREE OF KNOWLEDGE

The story of Creation in Genesis contains the item that represents mankind as having been condemned to eternal death as the consequence of our first parents' disobedience to God's command not to eat of the fruit of the tree of life and knowledge which is in the midst of the Garden of Eden. Here we are confronted with another of those features of the great allegorical drama of creation that has more than baffled the best efforts of theologians and scholars for two millennia. It provides another instance and example of the pitiful manner in which stupid attempt to interpret the Bible literally and factually has made of scholarship and Bible exegesis a laughing-stock and a mockery of sense and sanity for lo! these many centuries of Christian religionism. The story of how allegedly learned savants in the field of religious study have been misled and duped by the subterfuges of ancient methodology in the writing of sacred Scripture is one of the most astounding, indeed well-nigh incredible, narratives that, unfortunately, must now be told. It seems impossible to get across to the minds of clergymen and religious leaders today the simple truth that the ancient Bible writers did not commit themselves, as a writer does nowadays, to an effort to clarify their meaning in the simplest and most revealing language. Bibles were not written for this purpose or with this end in view. They can almost be said to have been attempts to hide, rather than to disclose, the truth they aimed to tell. For the purpose was not to broadcast for millions of readers (we must remember that there was no printing in the world then) the truth that was to be expressed, but rather to embalm for the sake of preservation a body of basic truths of life, religion and philosophy that might be lost if not thus edited.

The ancient method was based on a now completely lost and unknown literary practique. Instead of writing treatises in ordinary language, the aim was to put truth in the form of representations or pictures of it, such as dramas, allegories, myths, parables, fables, apologues, number graphs and pictographs on the star clusters in the sky. The pictorialization of truth was the work of dramatists rather than of plain prose expositors. The elements in man's nature, that were the real actors in the drama of his life, were made personal in the characters in the story, just as in Snow White and the Seven Dwarfs Snow White represents the pure divine nature in man, his soul, and the Dwarfs personify the seven elementary principles that build up his physical body and thus serve her in all mechanical ways.

The archaic method was designed to dramatize truth, not to write elaborate dissertations upon it. The genius which strove to construct the formulas that expressed the forces and processes of life was dramatic genius, not specifically literary genius in the modern sense. When neither writing nor reading was universal the only practical way to portray ideas was by pictorializing them in an allegory, myth, or a construction that might appear outwardly fantastic to an ignorant person, but would nevertheless subtly intimate to deeper intuition the forms of mighty truth. The sagacity that dictated such a methodology took in the recognition that for the mind of childhood a pictorial representation would not only convey for the moment, but impress in perpetuity, the idea designed to be taught. Much as the housewife puts up in jars the fruits to be preserved, the myth-makers and the dramatic poets (and the word "poet" means "a maker") embalmed in myths and dramas and a variety of concrete formulations the great ideographs of recondite wisdom which they transmitted to early humanity for its guidance throughout evolution. What the individual learns in his childhood serves him throughout life, for the memory of childhood is everlasting. It is the same with humanity in its infancy. The early races were all given the systems of moral and spiritual philosophy, done in myths and dramas, so that the graphs of living truth should never be wanting for human instruction in wisdom. The evidence is mountain high that all early peoples were the beneficiaries of essentially the same original body of sage wisdom, and that this primal deposit was the one unitary source of all the world's religions. They are thus proven to have been the "one true religion" at the start. By recovering that deposit the greatest need of the world today could readily be met,—a universal religion for all mankind. Towards this desirable consummation the present series should contribute no mean impulse, since its articles will come close to reconstructing in toto the outlines and substances of that mighty truth of old time.

NATURE'S BOOK OF REVELATION

The Tree of Knowledge was one feature of that great formulation that depicted truth in graphs and symbols. The Sages of antiquity did not have far to go to find not only apt and felicitous, but absolutely inerrant types, symbols and mimeographs of the cosmic laws and principles they had in mind to picture forth. The tools and instruments for truth's portrayal lay right at hand, or right outside the door. They were present in multitudinous form in the world of living nature. The sky, the earth, the ocean; vegetation and animal life; the universal daily phenomena of natural forces supplied the materials able to clarify the speech of truth. These ancient dramatists knew a fact that we are largely ignorant of,—that the processes and phenomena of creatural life are everywhere themselves the pictorial dramatizations of universal verity. They knew that every tree, bush, insect, worm, beast, every tumbling rill upon the hillside, every cloud, snowflake, mist and rainfall, was each in its way a visible delineation of cosmic principle. For these processes and creations were themselves the outward visible manifestation of the Soul of the Universe that was working to give itself concrete expression in myriads of variant forms. They were themselves truth come alive in the actual world. They were Universal Spirit's ideas that were now crystallized in material form in the outer world. They were God's archetypal ideas concreted in atomic matter, as an architect's ideas become substantialized in brick, mortar, wood, stone and iron. And precisely so. God, the great Architect, first formed in his cosmic mind the shape of things to come in his purposed new creation, and it was over their ideal pattern that he later formed the physical universe. In our benighted ignorance today we deride the idealist. But unless the individual is at all times striving to build his life in conformity with the pattern of a noble ideal, he will get nowhere except possibly to that bourne of all aimless drifting, or to the asylum over the hill. Psychology tells us now in tones we dare not disregard, that minds break down because of their want of aim, purpose and meaning in the struggle of life. Bizarre and almost ridiculous as it sounds in the ears of modern people, it can be said truly that philosophy is and must ever be man's true savior.

But the sublimest truths and ideals are pictured to us ubiquitously in the commonest things in nature. Possibly the commonest things in the world are trees. Just because this object is so common, it must be presumed to embody universal ideation in truest form. It does so indeed. When nature tells a story it can not be false, it can not lead the mind astray. Nature can tell nothing but the truth, because it is truth itself come to view in the actual world. Philosophers have argued for ages whether the actual things such as trees, rocks, streams, are real things, or only the appearance of real things. The whole visible world of things may be an illusion of man's mind, they contend. The obvious truth is that these things are indeed the appearance of real things, for they have emerged from the invisible world of noumenon or divine thought and made their appearance in this outer world of actuality. They were not, however, mere appearance in the sense of being an unreal semblance or ghost or shadow of reality, as has so generally been the way of describing them. They were the forms of reality itself, arrived at actualization in our world. Philosophy needs to make this vital correction in its thinking. Anything that is must be real. The philosophical dispute over reality or illusion is only a matter of relativity, contingent upon the level of consciousness that is present to evaluate reality. Anything is real to that level of consciousness that can cognize it, but real for that level and not for other levels. A radio wave at eight hundred is real for the receiving instrument set to catch that frequency. It is not real for a different set of the dial. Man—and the philosophers—had better settle this question of reality on the basis of naive acceptance, that our experience here is real. This world is real, terribly real, for us. It may not be real for cherubim and seraphim; but that should not mislead us, as it has done some misguided "spiritual" religionists in our own day and all past days, into thinking we can treat this world as unreal. Along that ideological path lie the whitened bones of many a wrecked personality, philosophically and psychologically speaking.

THE BRANCHING TREE OF LIFE

The tree, as symbol, tells the story of life with marvelous completeness and vivid explicitness. In its shape and configuration it is almost a picture itself of the structure of the cosmic creative plan, and it is a true picture of man's ideological conception of the form and modus of life manifestation. If one were to try to diagram the processes of creation, one's pencil would almost find itself tracing a figure that would much resemble a tree. Why? Because one would have to draw a heavy line out from a plane of rootage or origin, like the ground, representing the one first and undifferentiated stream of creative energy, and then branch it out into two streams and again divide these and their branches and branchlets into ever-multiplying separation and division. For that is precisely how the creative impulse emerges from its basal center and branches out into numberless arms and lines of force, to permeate at last the whole area of the universe it is to create.

The tree and the river were the two most apt and frequently used symbols of the outflow of living energy in creation. The one so vividly depicted the emanation of the life stream from one undivided source and the subsequent dividing and branching; thus typifying the emanative or involutionary direction of life outward at the beginning of a creative period. The other equally graphically symbolized the return or evolutionary direction from the many terminal streamlets back into the one main channel and the universal ocean. For the tree emanates from the ground as one shoot, to divide later into many. The stream begins from multitudinous rills and springs and ends by reuniting them all in the common sea. When typological genius wishes to show that the two forces of life, the outgoing and the returning, conjoin and intermingle their energies in the worlds of manifestation—as they do in man's sphere and in his body—they represented the two as working together. Speaking of the righteous man, the beautiful language of the Bible says: "He shall be like a tree planted by the river of water." The Solomon's Seal, or interlaced double triangle of esoteric symbolism is a monograph of this interrelation, as the one triangle points downward, the other upward. The downward direction represents the descent of soul into matter, the upward typifies the return back to infinite spiritual source. The Nordic mythology, however, pictured the two directions by portraying the great Tree of Life, Ygdrasil, as both rooted in earth, reaching up to heaven, and also rooted in heaven, extending its arms downward to earth. Involution brings life downward and branching out toward and upon earth; evolution takes it back to the empyrean. The banyan, and less visibly, other trees exemplify both directions. Any tree goes down to earth as seed or shoot, and returns to heaven as developing body.

Thus the tree, along with the stream, was employed by the ancient mythicists of divine truth as the symbol of first, the distribution, and then the reuniting of the living rivers of creative power that, like the four in Genesis, issued forth from the being of God and retuned to him. The magnificent Greek esoteric philosophy—the suggested revival of which can be the answer to the world's great cry for humanitarian culture today—represented the gods, who are the long arms and agents of God's own working energy, as being the "distributors of divinity". No phrase could be more enlightening for our dull powers of comprehension. Jesus says:

"I came to send fire over the earth," and he later, illustrating his meaning by breaking a loaf of bread into pieces and distributing one to each of his disciples, declared that he was breaking his body into fragments so that a piece might be distributed to each. Again he exemplified this division in "multiplying" the loaves and fishes to feed the enhungered multitude. All this was drawn to illustrate the great and forgotten principle of the ancient "divine theology" that the rays and streams of creative force that flow forth from the heart of God issue first as one undivided stream, then break and divide endlessly to reach and supply every nook and cranny of being in the universe. The Greeks called these streams of formative power "rivers of vivification". They start out from heaven as one undifferentiated current and reach the periphery of creation in countless branchlets. Then, having gone out and done their work of "watering all the face of the ground," they, precisely like the capillaries of our own blood system, turn back from their numberless end springs and begin to merge the many into fewer, and finally end in the One from which they emanated. If that does not picture to the mind even of the dullest the methodology and processes of God's creative work, it is hard to conceive how we can be taught obvious truth.

It is interesting to learn of the particular trees which the Sages chose as typical of creative mode. The northern nations used the ash and the pine, the latter because of its thrilling suggestion of the soul's immortality by its remaining ever-green in winter, the period of "death". The Druids, as well as the Greeks, used the oak. Mediterranean and Eastern religions used variously the palm, the olive, the banyan, the pine, tamarisk or tamarind or tamarack, the fig, the boddhi, juniper, cypress, cedar, ilex, persea, locust or acacia (the sacred tree of Masonry), and the fig under the name of sycamore. (Massey calls it the sycamore-fig.) Revelation speaks of two witnesses, whom it calls the "two olive trees". Egyptian texts speak of the "two divine sycamore trees of heaven and earth," a most revealing nomenclature indeed, since the description enables us at last to know what these two witnesses or the "two trees" in reality connote. They are now clearly seen to be the two streams of living power, the one emanating from heaven, the other rising up from earth, whose correlated work carries life through each of its great cycles. The one witness is the stream of involution flowing forth, the other the stream of evolution flowing back,—carrying its gains with it. The

mysterious sealed meaning of many a text in the Bible has had to wait these two thousand years for the discovery of the Rosetta Stone (1796) to supply the key to a lost interpretation. Egypt will redeem a decadent Christianity and its baffling Bible. The time for Christian scorning of "paganism" is past.

THAT "FORBIDDEN" FRUIT

There is now to be sought the solution of the perplexing dialectical problem involved in the conventional, time-honored and orthodox, but not rationally intelligible, theological propositions based on the Genesis verses which seem to declare that man was forbidden by divine command to eat the fruit of the tree of life and knowledge. Language is incompetent to convey any adequate realization of the damaging stultification of wholesome common sense which the utterly bungled and garbled distortion of the purport of this supposed divine ordinance has inflicted upon Western mankind over many centuries. The "forbidden fruit" and man's alleged disobedience to God in the eating of it and the penalty incurred for all humanity thereby have become bogies of Frankenstein proportions, charging the general conscience of the Occidental world with a paralyzing obsession of wonder, doubt, fear and vicarious remorse for all too many ages. The psychological devastation and havoc wrought upon sensitive minds indoctrinated from childhood with this baneful conception is past all calculation. Its doleful preeminence in the center of the West's structure of theology amply justifies its place in the first three lines of Milton's great epic:

> "Of man's first disobedience, and the fruit
>
> Of that forbidden tree whose mortal taste
>
> Brought death into the world and all our woe."

Gruesome and blighting have been the fatalistic implications of the theological legend that the eating of the fruit of a tree—in literal sense—by our "first parents" caused the "fall" of man and fastened upon the race of their descendants for all the future the penalty of expulsion from a land of Paradise and a life of toil, pain and sorrow upon the earth, with death the inevitable casualty in the end. It has lurked in the murky shadows of the Western subconscious, a threat to happiness and a rasping brake upon the natural joyous zest for life. Only the robust rebuff to the theological imposition by the natural hearty strength of man's instinctive sense of the preciousness of life, in spite of the deadening power of miasmatic religious misconceptions, has reduced to some mild extent the crushing consequences of the falsification. Had the West been disposed to subjective introversion as was the East, the fatal aftermath of its blind addiction to a weird and macabre theology such as that haunting prevalent belief, would have been catastrophic beyond all credence. It would have sunk the Occident in a morass of morbidity that would have sickened its whole moral psychology. Indeed to a degree not commonly glimpsed it has actually done just this, in spite of all the West's aggressive objectivity and extraversion of view. Protagonists of other religions, debating with Christianity, could well say that Christianity is the religion that has afflicted its devotees with the conviction of universal sin, and that without reference to the sinner's merit or demerit. It has convicted them of sin before they were born.

What the psychological resultant of such a general persuasion and infatuation on the minds of billions of people over the generations since Bethlehem could be, and tragically has been, the modern revelations of the science of Psychoanalysis are well prepared to inform us. This science asserts that for every depressing mental influence we have to pay a heavy penalty in the form of inhibitions, neuroses, pathologies and wretchedness grievous to contemplate. The enormity of this psychic bill is beyond estimate.

This cultural catastrophe is all the more unaccountable because there are other verses and clear statements in the Bible that virtually contradict or flatly controvert every implication of the divine command as theology has taken it. Reason and philosophy should of themselves have intimated to any thinking mind that God could not in simple consistency place man in a garden of life and then forbid him to eat the fruits of its living experience. Tragic mistake on a world-wide scale could have been averted if human reason had not been subverted by doctrinal obsession. With life given, and knowledge the certain fruit of its experience, a modicum of logical thinking could have assured the reason that God's alleged command at once convicted him of dialectical inconsistency. It accuses him of both giving man life and forbidding him to live it in the same breath. How could it be seen as compatible with itself that God would place man in the world of life, order him to grow and multiply, and then deny him the right to partake of the fruit of his experience, and predominantly of the fruit of that one tree that yields life and knowledge, both inevitable and indispensable to his increase and multiplication?

The artistry of ancient allegorism caught the world at a low point of its intelligence and mired the interpretative mind in Christianity in the worst slough of misconception ever to afflict the human fancy. Our dullness of comprehension and blank stupidity in handling our great heritage of ancient mythicism have marred and scarred the face of history.

But if reason failed to avert the mental cataclysm, there are things in the Bible which should have counteracted the direful aberrancy. If the eating of the fruit of the tree of life is seemingly forbidden in the third chapter of Genesis, it is, on the contrary, expressly asserted as man's right in the last chapter of the Bible. The Book flatly contradicts in its last chapter what it seems to say in its first ones. The 14th verse of the final (22nd) chapter of Revelation runs as follows: "Blessed are they that do his commandments, that they may have right to the tree of life, and may enter in through the gates into the city." Here man's right to eat of the tree is enunciated in forthright terms. Likewise one does not find anything like forbiddance in the statement in the Bible that "the leaves of the tree shall be for the healing of the nations". Unfortunately the illuminating power of such a verse has been dimmed by the ignorance of all that this tree is the same one as that in the garden. All this sad mental mishap has come from failure to know that the Bible is beautiful allegory and not weird and eccentric "history". Allegory talks of but one tree, for symbols carry but one specific connotation. History would argue that this tree of the healing leaves was another tree. It would even try to locate it somewhere on some mountain or in some valley, as it has tried to locate the garden itself in the Euphrates Valley. Just in passing one can mention the sacred tree of Tibetan lore, called Mani-Koum-Boum, or the "tree of the ten thousand precepts". It was asserted that on the under side of every leaf was written a golden precept of religious truth. One reads that it stood on the temple ground in some locality. That such a figure to cover splendid truth should have led minds into egregious folly is pitiable. An astute mind with a moment's reflection can see that it is a dramatization or symbolization of the very great truth that the forces of life branch out into living expression, and that each factual experience, poetized as one leaf on this mighty tree, unfolds its own moral lesson, or precept, for the creature living it! The fantastic literal idea corrupts and diseases the mind, the allegorical redaction of it frees and sanifies it. Tolstoi, the great Russian, in 1911 had a remarkable vision of the Balkan wars and the first world war, all of which was accurately fulfilled. One of the features of his vision still to come to reality was that he saw religion saving itself by returning to symbol and allegory. The early learned Christian Fathers urged the allegorical interpretation of the Scriptures! Later and less learned ones excoriated and anathematized them. The result of the latter blunder is only too inexpressibly apparent in a million forms of mental delusion and psychological wreckage under our eyes in history past and present.

The recondite elements of the allegory have utterly miscarried and piteously misled the credulous minds of religionists for these many centuries. The tree of life is the branching stream of living experience, and the gods sent man into this mundane milieu expressly to partake of its fruits to the full measure of his capability. The conception of the forbidden fruit in its gross theological and popularly accepted form, it must be said, is close to the most outrageous delusion of human belief ever to snare man's gullible fancy.

The sentence in the last chapter of Revelation completely upsets the idea that first man violated divine law or disobeyed God in the garden. It asserts man's right to eat of the tree's fruit.

Representations and vignettes found in ancient documents picture the scene of the "temptation" in the garden. There is the tree, with the woman standing close beside its branches, the serpent reaching out its head from the foliage and whispering into her ear, while she hands a cup of the juice of the fruit of the tree to her husband at her side. It is the allegory done over in vignette.

THE JUICE OF THE FRUIT

What the juice of the fruit of the tree signifies is most necessary to understand if one is to discern the full relevance of every item of the symbolism. It is glaringly obvious and there is no excuse for its having been missed for so long, to the universal detriment of mankind. What is fruit juice? It is the liquid essence which is forced out under physical pressure, and contains in it the inmost essence of the fruit's powers of nourishment. This description adumbrates for us a large segment of the meaning of all experience. It hints volubly at the great fact that all life is constituted of finer essences contained within coarser shells, and needing to be expressed (out-pressed) through the pressure of life's physical circumstance. In the tree there is the hard exterior, then the fluid sap and within that the vital essence. Matching this in man, there is his gross outer physical body, within that the blood, and in that, as we know, the pranic electricity of life. All of this furnishes us with an analogy with experience itself. Externally our experience consists of physical acts, states and phenomena, first. But a step farther inward it consists of conscious reactions to the crude physical contacts; first sensation; then, a step inward, emotion; another step inward, and as the result of sense and emotion, thought is generated; and still going inward, there is aroused at last the final spiritual being of the man in an assertion of will and purpose, the ultimate response.

Now it requires a vast quantity of outer experience to reach deeply within and deposit its final effects upon the innermost soul, and, so to say, squeeze out its spiritual reaction. Just as it takes hundreds of tons of crude coal to produce by distillation an ounce of sublimited power in radium form, so it takes vast quantities of crude physical, sensual and emotional experience to generate in the depths of being one single dynamic realization, one single flash of more splendid light, in the profoundest depths of consciousness. It is a most edifying analogy and a true one.

The most sublimated and hence most precious essence of the meaning and the good of man's conscious experience must thus be forced out to realization under pressure of vast amounts of outer sensual experience. Of this process and phenomenon the squeezing out of the juice of the fruit of a tree is the perfect analogue and outer type.

The juice of the fruit of the tree of life and knowledge is therefore to be sensed in a powerful mental way and understood as the ultimate soul reaction, or deposit in consciousness, from the whole process of mortal existence. Man partakes of this life-giving nectar, this wine of life, just insofar as his experience presses upon him with sufficient force to draw out from his deepest soul its divinest reactions.

And now comes a startling release of lost truth, impressive and significant enough in itself to cause a furore in religious circles. It is beyond dispute that the cup of this living essence, this sap of the tree of life, this juice of the fruit of the living tree of creation which the woman offers to the man in Genesis, is the same cup which the Jesus character in the New Testament, in his agonizing cry from the cross, pleads that his Father may let pass from him! After the first shock of its revelation, this statement should not be considered as either so strange or so unlikely, when another release of forgotten truth and another astonishing denouement of a correct following of symbolism, brings up beside it the similar pronouncement, even more revealing, that the Tree of the creation garden is the same tree as that on which Jesus was crucified! "Him whom ye slew and hanged on a tree" is one of the Bible passages which uses the word "tree" instead of "cross". It is not known that there are extent many old legends of ancient days in which the tradition was kept alive that the cross of Golgotha was cut from the wood of a tree which had been propagated from a branch, seed or shoot of the Tree of Paradise. Legend has sometimes preserved truth more securely than written Scripture. It is markedly so in this case.

When the allegorical-symbolic nature of ancient Biblical composition is better known, there will be no question that the Christ was crucified on the Tree of Life. As this tree keeps on unfolding its growth throughout the lengthy cycle, obviously the Christos must be represented as being crucified on its continuing fresh propagations from generation to generation.

Likewise Jesus was tempted by Satan, "that old serpent" of Revelation; and so we have four central items of the same story, the tree, the cup, the serpent and the temptation, in both the Genesis and the New Testament formulations of the archaic typology. These marks of identity between the two sweep aside all possible chicanery that has been resorted to to hold them apart as separate and different historical episodes! The certification of this identity constitutes a revelation and a revolution of gigantic proportions in all religious systemology. It renders obsolete at one stroke a whole vast mass of theological lucubration, heavy and sodden, that has deplorably misconceived and misrepresented the true and luminous meaning of the fabric of theology. The benignant rays of a new dawn of light and understanding break above the horizon with this announcement.

THE WILY SERPENT

Equally revolutionary in its significance must be seen to be the next point of exegesis,—that of the identity of the character of the "serpent" in the drama. The grand enlightenment which the creation story was designed to give the world has been sadly bedimmed by our sheer inability properly to identify the characters enacting the great cosmic scenario. In ecclesiastical religion not a word has been uttered in centuries that would give the remotest intimation as to the true reference of this subtle villain of the creation piece. Still the ignorant gape and their wonder grows as to why God, omnipotent and all wise, allowed a snake to come in to annoy the first human pair and so quickly seduce them to their—and our—eternal "fall". Common reasoning suggests that it was a bit unfair and inconsiderate of the Almighty Father to throw a giant temptation in the way of our first progenitors at the very first moment of their career. One must think that he should at least have given them time to get their bearings and learn by experience the operation of his divine laws for their guidance, before bearing down on them with a stern and grim prohibition, with their eternal destiny dangling on the issue.

Common credulity and as ignorant seminary tutelage have assumed that, from all the surface intimations of the story, the crafty serpent was the arch enemy of God and a fell plotter against his good work. Corrected understanding must clear this dramatis persona of both wicked plotting and enmity against the Supreme. One of the very first sects of early Christians was that of the Ophites, who "worshipped" the serpent (Greek: ophis) as their prime symbol. A naive mistaught Christian would from this jump to the conclusion that these Hebrew Christians must have been of the status of savage tribesmen under the horrid delusion that their God was the serpent. But we can see that if even Moses raised up the serpent on the cross in the wilderness, acting assumedly under God's control, that in some fashion or other this fearsome reptile must have stood as symbol of something on the good side of the meaning.

Ordinary familiarity with the serpent symbol of ancient literature, especially of the uraeus-snake of the Egyptians, and a wiser study of comparative religion, would have obviated the world-wide and age-old blunder of mistaking the serpent for a hostile element in the work of creation. People have been puzzled, after reading the stories of the evil serpent, to hear the Divine Teacher in the New Testament enjoin upon his followers to "be wise as serpents". Popular Christian belief has surely reduced the mythical representations of great cosmic truth in its own Scriptures to a mélange of incomprehensible oddities.

The graphic and vivid instructive significance of this animal symbol inheres in the suggestive hints and analogues which the creature supplies to thought. Sagacity in olden times quickly caught at a quite thoroughgoing analogy between its shape, its characteristics and life habits, and the general form of evolutionary processes themselves. Its length of body, permitting it to coil, in general spiral shape, around seven folds, with its head rising at the top or culmination, furnished a striking picturization of the great creative force itself. Like the serpent, this energy swings ever seven times around its great and lesser cycles, and erects its culminating product, which is clearly enough the higher consciousness centering in the head, at the topmost point of attainment. The snake lying coiled seven times round on itself formed a circular central hole, which was called by the Greeks "the snake's hole", or the Cycle of Necessity (kuklos anagkes—the Kukl-os becoming cycl-e in English). This was to emblemize the inescapable necessity of the soul's swinging seven times through the rounds of the elements to gain its evolutionary growth.

The serpent, then, accurately typifies, and as a dramatic figure in the allegory, represents the great Cyclic Law, or Law of Evolution, which takes all creatural life swinging eternally round the seven-ringed cycles of incarnation in lower grades of matter. Without this immersion in matter's depths and the increase in growth accruing therefrom, the soul could not further evolve. The serpent symbolizes, therefore, the wholly beneficent law of life itself. As nearly as we can paraphrase it in modern parlance, the serpent is just the "natural law".

But now, as, for the sake of dramatic representation and the accentuation, for weak human ideation, of the difference in cosmic rank, and opposition of function, between the automatic natural law of physis, (as the Greeks called it) and the higher spiritual law of the divine mind, the first being, as with us, God's subconscious activities, and the second his conscious directing intelligence, the dramatists painted the crawling reptile that carried the symbolism of the lower automatism in the colors of (comparative) evil. The two laws, the natural and the spiritual, operating jointly in man's nature, do stand in contrariety, even in a sense in opposition to each other. But thousands of years of fatuity and folly have been the product of the failure of theological acumen to evaluate this opposition in its true measure and proportion of balanced understanding. The gross misconception to which all ancient symbolization of high and abstruse truth has been subjected and by which it has been mutilated into a veritable travesty of its true interior sense, has wrought havoc with the original high purport of the construction. It has mistaken the opposition of relation, position and function, for the opposition of moral and spiritual design and purpose. It has mistaken the opposition of polarity for the opposition of good and evil. Or, it has misconceived the opposition as of right and left, lever and fulcrum, symmetry and balance, fingers and thumb, for the opposition of evil to good. It has taken one of the two opposing arms of being that uphold the worlds and, abstracting it out of its relation to the whole process, declared it to be evil. All work, including all creative work, is accomplished by the mutual exertion of force against resistance and of resistance against force. And what folly for philosophers so far to forget themselves as to fall into the error of calling the resistant force evil, because it seems to be blocking the effort of the working force! Both are equally necessary and are therefore equally beneficent and good. They are the two halves of total being. It is their function to balance, to stabilize and finally to actualize the values their tension brings to birth. If one of them failed to stand up to its nature and function, the other would collapse with it immediately. It is the pull and attraction between the two that upholds the universe. Their cooperation is that of function and instrument, purpose and means, and it is required that they take their places at opposite ends of the polarity and provide for each other the resistance that alone would stabilize their activities at given times and locations in the cosmos. No more is the opposition of matter and spirit evil than is the opposition of man and woman, darkness and light, heat and cold. Life could not advance to higher ends in its unfoldment if the two ends of the everlasting polarity were not opposed to each other and countervailing against each other. They are opposed to each other; yes, in sheer mode of function, but certainly not opposed in ultimate aim and goodness.

Reckless misconception of the opposition of polarities has introduced into all religion the most damaging eccentricities of belief and conduct perhaps ever recorded on the weak side of human ideation. The story is too gruesome and horrifying to recount. It has caused billions of minds to live under the darksome shadow of the presupposition that nature, the world, the flesh, the very body of man—as against his soul—the natural functions and desires, the very enjoyment of man's life in the body, are all foul forms of evil. It has led millions in all ages to attempt to crush and mortify the natural bodily side of their lives. (A later work will deal exhaustively with this feature.)

It is so deeply interwoven into the texture of the present essay in relation to the tree of knowledge that it had to be given cursory introductory treatment. It can be seen that the ability of man's philosophical sagacity to discern rightly the very truth here expounded, and so to balance his life between the two functional pressures of the good and the evil, as these are seen in the common human view, and to realize that ultimately all things, in spite of appearances to the contrary, are working together for his good and are good in themselves, understanding them as the good divided into its bipolar aspects of function and instrument, balancing, not thwarting each other,—this ability of man to achieve one aspect of this balance in the conceptual realization that the opposition of the two is wholly beneficent and salutary, is itself one of the prime goals of his life.

Hence it is woven into the story in the very name of the tree. The tree of life bears on its outermost branches the ultimate buds and blossoms and fruits of knowledge, which fruits consist of man's final attainment of the genius to know that both good and evil, as apparent to lower discrimination, become resolved in a higher synthesis of understanding, in which both merge into that which lies "beyond good and evil". But it takes the whole experience of life in earthly bodies—and, the ancients added, many such lives—to open the eyes of mortals to the perception of the non-reality of the apparent opposition between good and evil. So it was not until the human pair—themselves an expression of the polarduality—the "opposition" of man and woman—had eaten of the "forbidden" fruit that "the eyes of them were opened". For the serpent had expressed to the woman the very essence of the paragraph here written, that if they ate of the fruit of this tree, "then your eyes shall be opened, and ye shall be as gods, knowing good and evil."

Here is the clinching certification that man's deification, the distant goal and crowning achievement of his long course of evolution, comes with and through his rising in mind estate to the mountain-top of vision wherefrom he can see good and evil melt together in one transcendent consummation of beneficence.

THE TWELVE FRUITS OF THE TREE

Again the last chapter of the Bible supplements and illustrates the first ones. Nothing is more revealing than its second verse. The seer announces that the spirit has shown him the "pure river of the water of life, proceeding out of the throne of God and the Lamb". "And in the midst of the street of it, and on either side of the river, was there the tree of life, which bare twelve manner of fruits, and yielded her fruit every month; and the leaves of the tree were for the healing of the nations."

Hardly could there be found a more sublime delineation of the graph of man's historical existence and its scheme of unfoldment anywhere in poetic literature. The great stream of vivific creative energy flows forth from the highest or innermost seat of Being and nourishes the growth of this tree of constructive organic existence, man's creatural life among the rest. The most luminous item of the depiction is that the tree grows on either side of the river of water. In this single phrase, had esoteric penetration prevailed over stupid literalism, was to be seen the immediate rebuke and denial of all that vast sweep of pious religionism and alleged "spiritual" philosophy which elevated and worshipped spirit and equally deprecated nature, matter and body. For the tree has, and must have, its roots firmly grounded in both banks of the stream, the spiritual and the material. Here is truth that mankind sorely needs, and never so as now. The fate of religion, philosophy, human culture, hangs precariously in the balance until this point is certified in all thinking minds.

Genesis does not expressly say that the tree bears "twelve manner of fruits", but Revelation does. Again here is mighty instruction. Man, it was once known, is to evolve in his entire life course twelve distinct forms or faculties of higher consciousness, to which he will give full function as he becomes the god he is destined to be. This basic knowledge was the ground and origin of all the divisions of twelves in arcane literature and religious symbolism. It is generic for the twelve months of the year, the twelve hours (twice) of the day, the twelve tribes of Israel or sons of Jacob, the twelve disciples of the Christos, who were "shepherds" under the sign of Aries, "fishermen" under that of Pisces, the twelve stone pillars in ancient temples, the twelve lines of the four faces of the great pyramid, and many another twelvefold type of depiction. Men will be as gods when they shall have perfected these twelve unfolding aspects of divine Mind. The putting forth one of the twelve fruits each "month" is a further play on the symbolism of the evolutionary process, in which each cyclic period is thought of as producing its given spiritual product in regular order of growth.

THE HEALING LEAVES

The significance of the poetic assertion that "the leaves of the tree shall be for the healing of the nations" is of transcendent value; and again it has been missed by purblind religiosity. Why it is the leaves, and not the roots or trunk or branches, that are to heal mankind, is the point of keen allegorical reference that must be brought out. The instruction for us here lies hidden in the realization that the leaves are a periodical and distinctly cyclic manifestation in the life of the tree. They are projected seasonally on the outer body of the perennial and live and die in a regular periodicity. The life of the permanent body of the tree annually pushes out beyond its previous boundary and builds for itself a new extension of its body through which it can experience a new era of growth. The permanent soul of being must put itself forth to exercise in new embodiment constantly and recurrently. The soul of the tree has its seasonal experience in this transient vehicle, produces its fruit and withdraws at the cycle's end, appropriating the products of its annual activity in the leaf, but leaving the outer body of that leaf to wither and die off in the winds of autumn.

In the face of this eternally repeated demonstration of life's processes it is futile for stolid ignorance to deny any longer the methodology by which it carries the gains of one cycle over to use as capital in the endlessly following cycles. It speaks in unquestioned tones of affirmation of the universal ancient and early Christian thesis that spirit reincarnates in material bodies over and over till the day of its perfection in each cycle's range of teaching power. The Church violently threw out the doctrine in the sixth century at the Second Council of Constantinople, but it harbored it until that time. It would be well if this prominent fact of Church history were not so sedulously concealed.

The successive incarnations of units of spiritual Mind, which are the "Sons of God", individualized seed fragments of God's own consciousness, in bodies of physical matter on a given planet are indeed the "leaves" put forth by the tree of life season after season, and these incarnations and the experience they give the souls undergoing them shall truly enough be "for the healing of the nations". For only through repeated embodiment in such mundane vessels of flesh can the soul from God gain that long course of instruction and enlightenment that will eventually, through the opening of its eyes to truth, heal it of all the imperfections that limit and distress it because of its ignorance at the start. The tree is the Tree of Knowledge, and its twelve fruits are those twelve segments of complete divine understanding and mastery of life's deepest secrets. With such perfected wisdom will the men of the nations of mankind heal their infirmities and unfold their lives in beauty and happiness. How insistently the Book of Proverbs drives home the preciousness of knowledge, wisdom and understanding, asserting that they surpass in value all that the heart can desire. And specifically it says that they shall be "health" to the man possessing them. Only through continued incarnation can the soul rise to the point of knowledge which will enable it to free itself from all its ills.

The annual round of living activities of the tree form a perfect analogue of the similar activities of the tree of life in every higher and vaster sphere of being in the universe. We have lost the principles of the great illuminating science of analogy. The tree teaches us irrefutably and inescapably that a permanent and eternal part of life, namely the soul of divine consciousness, periodically puts forth into manifestation an arm of its power, which expresses itself in a cycle of birth, growth, maturity, decay and "death", appropriates to itself the increment of growth gained thereby, and withdraws into the invisible world of spiritual being at the end. If, then, man is made in the image and likeness of this cosmic pattern, it must be true beyond debate that a permanent and eternal part of him—his immortal soul—periodically puts forth a ray of its own power in order to relate itself to the forces at play in the material world, appropriates the harvest of many such repeated experiences and thus increases its own expansion into infinite divinity and glory of conscious being. The tree settles this debate beyond cavil.

WHY WAS MAN TEMPTED?

It is necessary next to extract from the allegory the hidden meaning of the puzzling item of the "temptation" of the women by the serpent and of the man by the woman.

This "temptation" has been another of the numberless characterizations designed to portray recondite truth that have caught the dullard intellect of the West in the toils of its cryptic subterfuge. People of incapacity for reflection have wondered without end why God, just and fair in his judgments (the "judgments of the Lord are true and righteous altogether"), would permit a "wicked adversary" such as the theological Satan, "that old serpent", to connive to torment his most righteous servant Job, and here in Genesis to scheme subtly to defeat God's own creative work in the formation of mankind. It has all come from the failure of philosophical acumen to catch the sane significance of the item of the opposition of polarities analyzed in an earlier paragraph. Due to this failure of insight there has been (mis)read into this term "temptation" a low human connotation of the word, which leaves the mind miles away from its intended significance. To "tempt" is to present to the intended victim or subject a lure, or prospect of an appealing or desirable nature with the hope that he may "bite" on it and thus fall into the designed trap set by the tempter. Common view at any rate has largely taken this form of understanding. A very minute element of this reference, perhaps, does inhere in the evolutionary situation which the Bible glyph is dealing with, but only in the most playful form. The real meaning concerns picturing cosmic procedure, all of which is intrinsically normal and good.

The word itself—temptation—comes either from the Latin tento, "to try", "to test", "to experiment with", or from tempto, "to tempt". It is likely that both these forms are but variants of one original root. In the first instance, if from tento, it would carry the meaning of "to give trial to", "to try out", in actual practice, "to test", or "to put to the test or trial". In this reference it would indicate that the "temptation" to which God subjects all his creatures—who are, be it remembered, the cells or members of his own body!—is nothing more nor less than his sending them out into incarnate life, his planting them in his gardens, that "they may have right to the tree of life" and grow by developing their latent capacities and powers through overcoming the "opposition" of inert matter in the duality of life. In the Book of Revelation the seven great rewards are promised to "him that overcometh". To grow to higher beauty Spirit must overcome the inertia of matter. Its aeonial victory can be gained only as the outcome of incarnational effort, continued until the goal is attained. So God's Sons must continuously reincarnate. This is to subject them to the tension that prevails between them and the force of matter. And this is the ordeal, the trial, the testing, the "tentation", as it might better be named. It has nothing to do with the theological "sin" of disobedience whatsoever. It is God's pathway for all his children, the natural beneficent course of his plan for their evolution.

If, on the other hand, the word derives from tempto, it stands related to an even more significant background of meaning. It would be revealed at once as being connected with the Latin word tempus, "time". To "tempt" man would then be to bring his soul down from the realms of spirit, where all religions have asserted that consciousness lies above the human apperception of time—where time exists not—and throw it under the illusion of the time sense. To "tempt" man would be to subject him to the time consciousness. This type of consciousness comes through the reduction of higher mind to a lower tempo of vibration as it falls under the limitations of brain activity. And it would be hard to pick a truer psychological definition of the situation confronting the soul in the Genesis recital than this very one here depicted. It is exactly what happens in the genesis of humanity, and incarnation does expressly subject the soul to a reduction to the time sense. So the "temptation" is just another glyph for the descent of the soul into mundane life, with the hidden accentuation on the sad diminution of the soul's powers under the trammels of the flesh. It is in the Greek philosophy of esotericism that one finds this rationalization of the soul's loss of divinity in exchange for human powers of consciousness so thoroughly illuminated. It in reality constitutes the loss of Paradise. For what is Paradise but a higher dimension of consciousness?

The "temptation", then, resolves back into the same thing that is otherwise indicated as the meaning of all those other forms of the experience of the Son of God on earth: his baptism, crucifixion, transfiguration. All these refer to but one thing, the incarnation. All are but facets of the career of the divine fragment of soul when imprisoned in mortal body, or just that career viewed from the various angles of its involvement.

Few have ever asked the question why the temptation came first from the serpent to the woman and from her to the man. Yet this procedure points to most significant understanding. The point is that the cyclic law tempts woman first, because "woman" typifies matter (the word "matter" is identical with the Latin word for "mother", mater), the eternal mother of all life, and matter is the first element visibly projected on the scene of creation. Matter, the mother, the "woman", is the embodiment of the first grades of life and consciousness in a cyclical round, and is therefore first on the scene. Matter must be produced and brought to organic form, so as to generate the highly complex mechanisms of brain and nervous system, ere consciousness and spirit, the male principles, can be brought to birth and function. The "mother" must have grown to adulthood in the vast cycles of time, before she can produce her Christly offspring of divine mind. So the Cyclic Law, the old, old serpent, involves "woman" in its toils first. It "tempts" her in the lighter sense of the word, because it offers to every atom of her body an infinite career of growth and expansion to the eventual crowning goal of self-consciousness. So the "woman" takes and eats first.

Then matter produces the element of soul as its son, and having in its old age of the evolutionary cycle prepared the organic bodies capable of registering the high vibrations of a soul's consciousness, it invites "man" (man is the Sanskrit verb meaning "to think"), the first thinker, to unite with it in partaking of the living experience and eating its glorious fruits. This all comports most harmoniously with the Bible's statement, already canvassed, that God formed man from the atomic dust, rendered as "the dust of the ground", which in effect says that God formed man from atomic matter, the "woman".

THE FRUIT LEADS MAN TO "DEATH"

Now since the Bible itself contradicts the popular conception as to the prohibition enjoined on man against eating of the tree of life, the great wonder arises as to how such an apparently direct and positive injunction found its way into the sacred text. This does not yield so readily to clear elucidation, yet the thesis here presented for the first time does provide the necessary elements of explanation. And this again constitutes an epochal disclosure.

It must be seen through the eyes of dramatism. These old formulations are dramatic allegories. The apparent, but by no means actual prohibition falls in because of a faulty way of transcribing the construction of the original story. It is possible, with the keys already in our hands, now to reconstruct the Genesis dialogue so as to see what a fuller account would have brought out in clearer focus.

What, then, has been taken to be God's interdiction of man's doing the very thing he was sent here to do must be reformulated so as to bring out what it was intended to convey—or more likely to conceal! The gist of the speech made by Kurios ho Theos (Lord the God) in which the fatal command was given, might be restated somewhat as follows: Here, Adam, the man, I have created you and placed you in the wonderful garden of life and consciousness. All the fruits of its many trees of thrilling experience you may eat. But the central and greatest tree of all is the tree of life and knowledge. This you will desire to eat; but I must make it clear to you: if you desire to partake of the fruit of this wondrous tree, you must suffer "death".

Now, the entire clarification of the exegesis rests upon our correct understanding of one word, "death", and its verb "to die". One of the later numbers of this series will deal with the lost theological meaning of these words. It has been already pronounced the most significant single revelation in religious study in modern times. Briefly put here, in anticipation of its fuller development in the later work, it may be stated that the Bible writers employed the words in that cryptic sense in which it was used in the Greek religious philosophy. There we find "death" used to denote the reduced state of the soul's life when it descended into the earthly body and became torpid and inert under the slower pulse of life's energies in the material worlds. Paul clearly states that the soul came under bondage to the law of sin and death "which is in our members" when in incarnation. In short ancient wisdom conceived and called the soul's life in mortal body its "death"—on the "cross" of matter.

Here, then, is our key to man's "death" coming with his "fall" in Genesis. Light shines at last. God laid down to his creatures the law of being, that under the irrevocable and inexorable Cycle of Necessity, if they wished to partake of all the largesse of his bounty in conscious life, they must know that it involved their descent into the valley of the shadow—of "death". It is as if he said: If you wish to gain all this wondrous life, you must first lose it, down in cyclical "death" in earthly body. To gain the distant heights of being you will have to cross the low valley, where the soul lies long buried in its earthly tomb. You will have to cross the blood-red sea of life in physical bodies, but I will be with you and the waves shall not overwhelm you.

One need not go outside the letter text of the Bible story itself to find the essential confirmation of the correctness of this reading. God issues his "command"—now better seen as a dramatized manual of instruction for his creature, man; and then the serpent, the Cyclic Law, has its rejoinder. Says it to the "woman" and through her to the "man": God has told you only that if you eat of the fruit of the tree of life and knowledge, you will surely "die". Now I must add that this is in reality not the death you think it is. Hear me further: I will give you the comforting assurance that if ye eat of this fruit, ye shall not die in any final sense; nay more, if ye eat of this fruit, ye shall from the eating thereof become as gods, knowing good and evil, for your eating will open your eyes to see all life with the understanding of gods.

And the revealing utterance of the serpent is his statement to Eve that "God doth know" that the eating will make you as one of the Elohim, who know the eventual beneficence of the tension between good and evil. Unless this rendition is accepted, exegesis faces the insoluble problem of reconciling a vast logical inconsistency, if not the most eccentric and irrational conduct on the part of omniscient Deity. If, as the serpent states, God knew that life for man would end in his elevation among the gods, which very goal he had set for man, on what logically consistent grounds could he have forbidden the creature the right to eat? Any other answer but the one here suggested argues undeniable whimsicality and caprice on the part of the all-just Creator. It must be seen that the entire orthodox Christian interpretation does thus rest on the accrediting God with gross and weird inconsistency. God can not offer man life and knowledge and then be reasonable in forbidding him to take them. Here has been a huge stumbling block in all Christian theology over the centuries. The plain common sense of thinking people detects this flaw—and wonders. It is questionable whether the allegory of the "forbidden fruit" has been clearly seen as a rational item by a single mind in Christendom. It has contributed its obscurantism to a hundred similar illogicalities to defeat the high good that religion and the sacred Scriptures could have rendered. It is time such things were corrected.

Then in the 22nd verse of the third chapter of Genesis the truth comes out! For there the drama has God saying: "Behold the man is become as one of us, to know good and evil: and now lest he put forth his hand and take also of the tree of life, and eat and live forever:

therefore the Lord God sent him forth from the garden of Eden to till the ground from which he was taken."

All hinges here on the conjunctive adverb "lest". It must be a sound argument that contends there may have been either deliberate tampering with the original text (as, to our disgust, we learn there has been all through religious history), or equally deliberate clever covering of the real sense by dramatic subtlety, which could be the more likely here. We can conceive the dramatist as desiring to veil the open sense by a playful ruse. Much as a rich and indulgent father, head of a great business concern, would offer his son full participation in the enterprise, yet at the start of the son's serious career, he would say to him: "You are to be one of us in the management, but lest you try to take hold of your prerogatives before you have mastered all the details of the business, to know the right from the wrong course of procedure, I must send you out into the factory to learn it all from the bottom up." This sums almost incontestably the gist of the logic of the situation, let the argumentative chips fall where they may. And it does bring out rational light, when all previous exegesis has left the matter shrouded in Stygian darkness. It may be the final basis of all sanity in our religious psychology to understand that even God can not give unto his beloved children the bliss and blessedness of divine life without imposing on them the ineluctable condition that they earn the right to it by developing the capability for it in the time-tempting mill of evolution.

And now, as a climactic denouement to the whole tragic muddle of centuries, comes the astonishing disclosure that all the while the confusion and misunderstanding prevailed, the words of the Bible text itself are found to have clearly stated that the "woman" was not gullibly victimized by a trap set by the wily serpent at all, that "she" made her choice to eat of the tree in full knowledge and realization of the consequences, understanding that "she" was making the wholly right and true choice in the situation. The old traditional sense of the temptation as disobedience to God's command and errant waywardness is directly shattered to bits by the actual wording of the story! For after the serpent had amplified the Lord's brief assertion that the eating would bring the "death" of incarnational existence, the narrative uses language which negates utterly the assumption that the "woman" was lured unwittingly into a trap. It says that "when the woman saw that the tree was good for food; and that it was pleasant to the eyes, and a tree to be desired to make one wise, she took of the fruit thereof." Here is no hint of deception and dupery, but deliberate intelligent choice, based on "her" own knowledge and observation. She acted on what "she" saw. "She" saw that the eating would eventuate in giving "her" and "her husband" wisdom. From every point of view it was overwhelmingly desirable. It meant a plunge into the waters of "death" and a long struggle with the serpent's forces, but not all of this was to be compared with that glory which should be its outcome. For the "death" on the cross of matter would be temporary, while the guerdon of the trial would be life and light everlasting. No other choice was possible to a mind that saw the eventualities, the risk and its enchanting reward.

FROM INNOCENCE TO KNOWLEDGE

Of the many trees denominated by ancient fancy as trees of life none was more generally prominent than the sycamore-fig. Particularly in Egyptian symbology was it outstanding as the Tree of Life. As the branches of the living tree that spread out their arms to erect the structure of life's expression clothed themselves with leaves each season, there is a reference to life clothing itself with fig-leaves in the creation narrative. Adam and Eve, finding themselves divested of their radiant spiritual garments, hastily sew together leaves of the fig tree to form aprons with which to cover their "nakedness". The obvious albeit esoteric reference is, of course, not to natural clothing, but to the outer physical bodies which the nucleus of spiritual soul puts on to give it contact with the lower planes. The tree is itself the broad picturization of life clothing itself in material body.

These considerations put us directly on the track of an explanation for the strange episode of Jesus stropping to curse the unfruitful fig tree in the New Testament. The tree is to bear the twelve manner of fruits on its branches. As the one noted by the Christ had not borne its fruit, the dramatist made a point of representing the failure as bringing the natural order under the "curse" of the divine Son. The Gnostic Christian literature laid great stress upon the failure of Mother Nature to bring forth the Sons of God, awaiting the coming of the Christ-Aeon, going so far as to denominate her effort "the great abortion". Of all this deeper sense the episode of the Christ figure "cursing" the fig tree is an analogue thrown off in a somewhat lighter vein of dramatism.

But there is deep relevance in this tree name "sycamore". The syc- root is most interesting. According to Massey it is derived from the same Greek root which gives the Greek word for "soul"—psuche (psyche). It is therefore the tree of soul, the tree which incarnates and typifies the life of soul.

It can be noted in passing, also, that the symbolic tree of Masonry, the locust-acacia, is another typal representative of the tree of Eden. For it is the Greek a-ka-kia (acacia), meaning "innocence", "harmlessness". The Edenic tree has often been called "the Tree of Innocence", indicating the condition of life in its pristine "purity", before its "fall" into matter, "death", and generation.

The tree is prolific in the fruit it bears for man's enlightenment merely through its analogical intimations. Aspects of these will be limned in succeeding essays; they are central in the work of interpretation. But one feature of analogy must be presented here. The tree bears its fruit through the intercourse of male and female organs out on the extremity of its numberless branches. So does the tree of life and knowledge. The creative streams permeate the worlds of matter as far as their initial impulse will carry them. They come to a standstill on the outermost rim of their movement; there they form a liaison with matter, they unite their energies with the powers latent there in the atom, and, impregnating those physical powers with the germs of mind, they give the initial impulse and direction to the evolutionary drive.

In actual fact life reaches the periphery of its creative sphere when its impulses have planted its seeds in the root soil of matter. Where the seeds are implanted growth naturally begins. Away out, then, on the farthest boundaries of its reach the tree of life bears its fruits. Here male and female potencies come to full and separate embodiment and through mutual attraction unite their father and mother capabilities for the generation of new life.

There is an impressive reminder of all this in the allegory of the gestation of the twin Jacob and Esau in the womb of their mother Rebecca. Theological dullness has been slow to catch the significance of the many pairs of twins or brothers (sometimes sisters) introduced into sacred literature the world over and plentiful in the Bible. They are even found in the astrological symbolism in the Gemini pair of the Zodiac. They represent—it could not be otherwise—the two nodes or poles of creative force, spirit and matter, or male and female creative potentiality (even when both are of one sex). These two forces are released or separated off from primal unity at the dawn of the cycle and swing apart into opposition, so as to balance the universe between them. Hence they are shown as fighting, the one generally "slaying" the other, as in the Cain-Abel instance. In the Egyptian allegorism they continue to "slay" each other in turn, over and over again. Here is the final proof that this "slaying" is only figurative. On the descent or involution of spirit into matter, matter is said to "slay" spirit; on the evolutionary return spirit overcomes matter. In the Jacob-Esau birth narrative (Gen. 25:23) the common features of the cosmic allegory are well limned. The two children "struggled together within her". And God explained: "Two nations are in thy womb, and two manner of people shall be separated from thy bowels; and the one people shall be stronger than the other people; and the elder shall serve the younger." The one, of course, is the material nature; the other is the divine spiritual Principle, in man's constitution the Christos. The elder is

Mother Nature, matter, "the first old Mother" of the Egyptian depiction. She is first on the scene of creation and is grown old before she gives birth to her Son, the Logos and its ray, the Christos. And nature serves the younger power of Mind, which is indeed born out of her womb.

In the New Testament there is a suggestive little allegory in which the tree is used to bring out one tiny aspect of significance. We have it in the words of the Massachusetts Bay Psalm Book:

> Zaccheus he
>
> Did climb a tree
>
> The Lord to see.

The story represents Zaccheus as so eager to see the Christ as he came by that to get above the press of the milling throng he climbed into a tree. The moral here is both obvious and charming. If one would see the Christos, amid the press and throng of worldly interests, one must climb pretty far up in the branches of the tree of evolving life, where the vision is not obstructed by the dense pressure of lower abstractions. Allegory is ever a sublimer teacher than history.

A study of the tree emblemism would not be complete without touching on the great religious tradition of the "golden bough". The tree of life was said poetically to bear on its topmost branch a bough of gold. The tree planted in the primordial garden, with its roots in heaven, its branches on earth, was in the course of the cycle to culminate in the production of a branch of shining glory. One of the names given to the Christ in the Bible (and previous literature) was "the Branch". Indeed the Hebrew word for "branch" is natzer, which is believed to be the base of the words Nazar-ene and Nazar-eth.

The tree of evolution is to end in the generation of the Christ nature in man, and when the Christ is generated the man is transfigured until "his face shines like the sun and his garments become white as the light". Oddly enough the words for light and for gold in the ancient books are practically identical throughout. Spirit is the great "golden light" of divine radiance. It is the refulgent aur,ar,or,ur,er of the various languages. When man's evolution terminates in the flowering out at its summit of the golden light of spiritual radiance, then indeed it has put forth its "golden bough". It is no wonder, then, that legend truly has it that the tree on which the Christ "died" for man's redemption, is a branch or shoot, or the wood, of the Tree of Life and Knowledge in the eternal Garden of Paradise. We are the fruit bearers on its earthly branches, and glory will be ours if haply we shall produce our topmost bough of golden light.

* * * * * * *

The tree has now contributed generously of its amazing symbolic light to our deeper understanding of hidden truth. Its trunk, branches, leaves, roots and fruit have carried home to reflective thought the priceless instruction they adumbrate. But it is a reflection that has come to few minds, that the fruit is at one and the same time both the end product of the cycle's growth and the beginning seed of a following cycle! In this startling realization of nature's marvels of economy lies buried the germ of perhaps the greatest of all mysteries of life, that end and beginning are one and the same thing, as they must be if life is to continue swinging round its endless cycles.

The mighty symbolism of the SEED will be the theme of the next elucidation,—THE ARK AND THE DELUGE.

The End.

39

Made in the USA
Monee, IL
09 March 2024